Rhythm

Clifford Bevan

Macmillan Education
London and Basingstoke

Contents

© Clifford Bevan 1983

All rights reserved. No part of this publication may be reproduced or transmitted, in any form or by any means, without permission.

First published 1983

Published by
MACMILLAN EDUCATION LIMITED
Houndmills Basingstoke Hampshire RG21 2XS
and London
Associated companies throughout the world

Designed and typeset by Oxprint Ltd, Oxford
Music setting processed by Halstan & Co. Ltd,
Amersham Bucks.
Printed in Hong Kong

ISBN 0 333 35416 8

Chapter one

Pulse

Using the first and second fingers of your left hand, find the pulse in your right wrist. If you haven't been rushing about, you will feel the steady, regular beat of your heart.

Doctors use an electrocardiograph to record a patient's heart-beats on a spool of graph paper. Each peak below represents a beat.

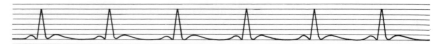

With your fingers on your pulse, follow the graph. Let your eyes move steadily from left to right, regulating the speed of their movement so that as they arrive at each peak you feel your heart-beat, or pulse.

Now take a pencil, and as your eyes again read from left to right at a steady pace, tap the head of the drum with the end of your pencil when you reach each peak.

You have just reproduced the PULSE or BEAT of your heart.

Crotchets and minims

Music also has a pulse, and the player of a musical instrument can reproduce the pulse that a composer has thought of in the same way as you have just reproduced your own heart-beat.

In ex. 1 each beat is shown by a musical note called a CROTCHET ♩

Reading steadily from left to right, once more tap the head of the drum with your pencil as your eyes reach each crotchet.

1

Music would be very monotonous if all the notes lasted for the same length of time. Read out loud the words of this old gipsy song:

> When it is raining
> The first thing in mind
> Is tent-rods and ridge-poles
> And kittle cranes to find.

Did you notice how you spent longer on 'mind' and 'find'?

We could show the lengths of the words in this poem, using crotchets for most of the syllables:

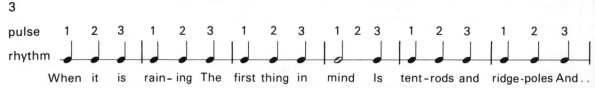

2 | When   it   is   rain - ing   The   first   thing   in . . .

Read these two lines again, tapping the head of the drum as you say each syllable.

The long word 'mind' lasts for two beats, and to show this we use a note called a MINIM ♩ . A ♩ lasts for one beat, and a ♩ lasts for two.

Read ex. 3 twice. First tap the beats and say the words, then just tap the beats while you count them in groups of three.

3

pulse   1   2   3   1   2   3   1   2   3   1   2   3   1   2   3   1   2   3

rhythm

When it is   rain- ing The   first thing in   mind   Is   tent - rods and   ridge - poles And . .

Notice that the **pulse** or **beat** stays constant (1 2 3) while the RHYTHM, the pattern of the notes, changes (♩ ♩ ♩).

When you are writing a crotchet or minim, draw the head of the note first ○ , then the stem │ . The minim's head is *not* round, but oval. Use two strokes ⟳ .

(A soft pencil, fine felt tip, 'Relief' nib, Osmiroid music pen or medium-straight italic nib are all good for writing music. If you use a pen with a nib, hold it so that the *down* stroke is fine │ and the cross-stroke is broad —.)

Accent

Why have we been counting in threes? Why not in fours or sevens? If you read out the words of *The Atching Tan Song* once again you will notice that we say certain syllables more heavily than others:

When it is *rain*ing The *first* thing in *mind* . . .

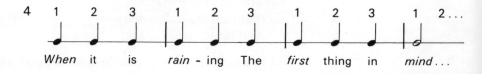

4   1   2   3   1   2   3   1   2   3   1   2 . . .

When   it   is   rain - ing   The   first   thing   in   mind . . .

Musicians say that there is an ACCENT on the syllables which are in italics. In this case the accents come at the beginning of each group of three beats, and we can group the notes in BARS, each containing a group of three beats. The end of each bar is shown by a BAR-LINE |

Semibreves

Sometimes the accents come at the beginning of each group of *four* beats.

Here is a well-known example:

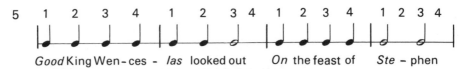

There is a very useful note called the SEMIBREVE o which lasts for four beats: it is as long as two minims or four crotchets.

Can you recognise the rhythm of this French folk-tune?

It is *Au clair de la lune*.

Time-signatures

At the beginning we put a TIME-SIGNATURE 𝄴 to show us the number and length of the beats in a bar.

The upper figure 4 tells us there are four beats in each bar.

The lower figure 4 tells us that each beat is a quarter of a semibreve in length – in other words, one crotchet.

In *Au clair de la lune*, then, each bar contains the equivalent of four crotchet beats.

A time-signature is *not* a fraction. There is no line between the two figures.

What would be the time-signature for *The Atching Tan Song*? Remember, there are *three* crotchet beats in each bar. Your reward for getting the time-signature right is to be let into the secret of what an atching tan is.

It is a stopping-place.

The following are time-signatures with a crotchet beat:

4/4 is called a	2/4 is called a
SIMPLE QUADRUPLE TIME	SIMPLE DUPLE TIME
3/4 is called a	4/4 is sometimes written
SIMPLE TRIPLE TIME	𝄴 COMMON TIME

Dots

$\frac{3}{4}$ presents us with a problem. We have a four-beat note (o), a two-beat (♩) and a one-beat (♩) note, but not a three-beat note.

We can overcome this difficulty by writing a DOT after a minim ♩. The dot equals half the length of the note it follows, so

♩. = ♩ + ♩ = 2 + 1 beats – in other words, 3 beats.

Here is an example of dotted minims in use.

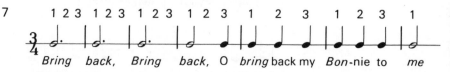

Bring back, Bring back, O bring back my Bon-nie to me

A dotted minim can also be used in bars containing other numbers of beats whenever a note lasting for three crotchet beats is required.

Quavers and semiquavers

Here are two other notes which are very useful:

The QUAVER ♪ is half the length of a crotchet.

Baa! Baa! Black sheep, Have you a - ny woo – l?

Baa! Baa! Black Sheep

The SEMIQUAVER ♫ is half the length of a quaver, or a quarter of a crotchet.

All peo - ple who have flab – by hands and ir - ri - tat - ing laughs

How quickly can you say this line from Gilbert and Sullivan's *Mikado*? You will find it helpful to look at the table of note values on page 13.

We can now write out our gipsy song in full. Notice the quavers for the word 'kit-tle', and the dotted minim at the end.

The end of a piece of music is shown by a DOUBLE BAR-LINE ‖

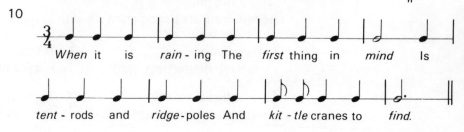

When it is rain - ing The first thing in mind Is

tent - rods and ridge - poles And kit - tle cranes to find.

Ties

The TIE or BIND is used to tie together two notes of the same pitch to indicate a sound equal in length to both of them combined. You could, for example, make a note three beats long either by dotting a minim 𝅗𝅥. or by tying a minim to a crotchet  tie

We use a tie when there is no other way of writing a note of the required length or when a note is held over a bar-line (see Chapter two).

More dots

Often a quaver is used with a dotted crotchet (𝅘𝅥. + 𝅘𝅥𝅮 = $1\frac{1}{2} + \frac{1}{2}$ beats).

11

All Through the Night

A quaver may itself be dotted. This makes it three-quarters of a crotchet beat in length, and a semiquaver can be used to make up the missing quarter beat, like this:

12

John Brown's Body

You may have noticed that the words of different verses of a song sometimes have slightly different rhythms. The last verse of this one begins

'He's *gone* to be a sol-dier in the *ar*-my of the Lord'

With the accents marked in italics, you will see that the first word, 'He's', comes *before* the first accent. We therefore need an extra 𝅘𝅥 before '*gone*'. The rhythm is then:

13

He's   *gone* to be   a sol-dier in   the   *ar* - my of   the Lord   — etc

Compare exx. 12 and 13.
We call the extra note at the beginning of the phrase an UPBEAT.

6

The upbeat plus the beats in the *last* bar of a piece of music should always add up to the number of beats in a complete bar.

Sometimes you will find two dots written after a note. This DOUBLE DOT adds to the note a half, and then a quarter, of its value. (The second dot represents half of the length of the first dot.) In other words, the length of the double-dotted note is increased by three-quarters. Here are some examples:

SINGLE DOT	DOUBLE DOT

Heads and tails

When notes with tails are side by side they are often joined by BEAMS, like this:

14

Baa! Baa! Black Sheep

Three or four notes with tails may be linked in this way, but they should be grouped in units of one beat:

15

Rossini: *William Tell* Overture

A note written on the five-line stave (see *Pitch and Melody*, Chapter one, The stave) normally has the stem turned up if its head is below the middle line, down if its head is on or above it:

16

Land of my Fathers

Rests

Music would be boring for the listener (and even dangerous for players such as trumpeters) if there were no periods of rest between the sounds. These silences are just as important as the sounds and are calculated as carefully as the lengths of the notes themselves. They are called RESTS. Each note has an equivalent rest.

NAME	NOTE	REST	COMMENTS
Semibreve	o	▬	4 crotchet beats (hanging from fourth line). Also used for a whole-bar rest, except in $\frac{4}{2}$ time (see page 9).
Minim	♩	▬	2 crotchet beats (standing on third line)
Crotchet*	♩	ξ	1 crotchet beat (in some older music you may find ⌐)
Quaver	♪	ꝛ	½ crotchet beat (don't confuse with ⌐)
Semiquaver	♬	ꝛ	¼ crotchet beat (same number of tails as the ♪)

Like notes, rests may also be dotted. It is best to use the longest rest possible: a minim rest is better than two crotchet rests, for example. But be careful to bear in mind that each half of a $\frac{4}{4}$ bar should be complete in itself.

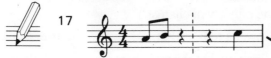

17

*Don't let anyone tell you that a crotchet rest is difficult to draw! There are four steps:

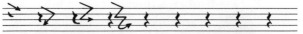

It's simply a letter Z with a sloping top sitting on a letter C. Keep your pencil on the paper the whole time you're drawing this rest, and note its position on the stave.

8

Hints on:

Add the correct rest(s) at the places marked with an asterisk.

Beethoven

STEP 1 Look carefully at the time-signature to discover the length of each beat.

STEP 2 Imagine lines dividing each bar into its separate beats.

STEP 3 Now check that each beat contains either notes, rests, or notes and rests adding up to its full length. (At this stage, that means the total length of each beat should equal a crotchet.) Pencil in any rests required. Add rests for any remaining beats in each bar.

STEP 4 Now read through the extract. You should find that it looks right and feels right. If it doesn't, check your pencilled rests to see why not. If it does – go ahead, and ink them in.

Other time-signatures

Sometimes it is easier for the composer to use a minim or a quaver as the main beat instead of a crotchet. (This does not necessarily mean that the speed of the music will change.)

In $\frac{3}{4}$ the lower 4 tells us that each beat is a quarter of a semibreve, i.e. a crotchet. To show that the main beat is a minim (half of a semibreve) the lower number would be a 2: $\frac{3}{2}$ – three minims.

What do you think the lower figure would be for a quaver? (Remember, a quaver is an eighth of a semibreve).

Here are three ways of writing *The Ash Grove*. You will notice that although they look different they all have the same rhythm and sound alike. (There is a table of all these time-signatures in Chapter four).

18

In the same way as there is a note equivalent to four crotchets there is also one for four minims. It is usually found only in older music and is called a BREVE ‖○‖

The breve equals 2 semibreves – 4 minims – 8 crotchets etc.

Time-signatures using minims as the main beat are called ALLA BREVE (Italian: 'by the breve') time-signatures. They were used most when the breve, not the semibreve, was the usual whole note (i.e. four beats). **Alla breve** time-signatures are therefore:

$\frac{4}{2}$ SIMPLE QUADRUPLE (4 beats in a bar)

$\frac{3}{2}$ SIMPLE TRIPLE (3 beats in a bar)

$\frac{2}{2}$ SIMPLE DUPLE (2 beats in a bar)

The time-signature $\frac{2}{2}$ is often written ¢ . Each bar contains the equivalent of 4 crotchets, as in C or $\frac{4}{4}$, but in ¢ there are only two beats – minims (not 4 crotchet beats).

In older music ¢ occasionally means $|♩\ ♩\ ♩\ ♩|$ ($\frac{4}{2}$).

Obviously you will have no problems in deciding whether there are two or four minims, or their equivalent, in each bar!

A whole-bar rest in $\frac{4}{2}$, or a rest of four minims, is shown by a breve rest ▬

Hints on: *Add the correct time-signature at the beginning of this extract.*

Beethoven

STEP I Identify each beat. The visual grouping of the notes will help you to do this, but also try to work out how they will sound.

STEP 2 For the time being, ignore any portion of a bar at the beginning of the extract. But when you have decided on the time-signature, add this portion to the incomplete last bar to check the total number of beats. They should add up to one complete bar.

STEP 3 If there are any ties, whether between notes in one bar or between two different bars, ignore them (in this example there are none).

STEP 4 Decide whether the beat is a crotchet, minim, or quaver. This will give you the lower number in the time-signature. The number of those beats in the bar will give you the upper figure.

STEP 5 You should now have decided what the upper and lower figures are. Do not be tempted to make the two figures into a fraction by adding a line between them!

STEP 6 Check through the extract again to make sure the time-signature is correct for the number and kind of beats in each bar.

Remember, when a melody begins with an incomplete bar, the final bar and the first, incomplete, bar should add up to a whole bar in length.

Triplets

19

Do you recognise this tune? It is a good one for marching. Try to sing or whistle the melody as you march round the room and notice its strong duple beat.

Many march tunes include not one, two or four notes to each beat, or step, but three. Can you think of any?

Here we come up against a problem: so far we have divided beats only into two, four, eight and so on, but not into three or six.

The way out of this is the TRIPLET. We simply write three notes to be played in the time normally taken by two.

Here is the framework of another march, ready and waiting for its tune.

The particular tune we are going to use includes three notes to one step, so we use a group of three quavers, or a **quaver triplet**, in the time usually taken by two quavers. These are written with a figure 3 above and are grouped together by a slur.

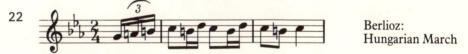

Now try marching to this tune and see how the three triplet notes fit into one step. The march has the same strong duple beat as ex. 19.

Quaver triplets (three quavers   in the time of two) are

the most common, but **semiquaver triplets** are found too:

Berlioz:
Hungarian March

These are often used to cope with three quick notes in a run up to a melody, or perhaps for ornamentation during the course of the music.

Delibes: Ballade

Crotchet triplets (which have their 3 written with a square bracket, not a slur) can seem majestic and impressive.

Debussy: *La mer*

Compound time

Sometimes there are so many triplets in a piece that it begins to look extremely complicated. Look at this march by Sousa, for example. Note that triplets can be broken down into their constituent parts, just like other beats, with notes or rests of corresponding value included.

25

It would be much easier to read if each **beat** were divided into three, so there would be six quavers (the two triplets) or their equivalent in each bar.

26

The time-signature would then become $\frac{6}{8}$. (The upper figure 6 tells us that there are six units in the bar and the lower figure 8 indicates that each unit is an eighth of a semibreve in length, i.e. a quaver.)

27

Sousa: *The Liberty Bell*

Remember, there are still only *two* beats in each bar, each divided into three quavers.

A time in which each beat divides into two is called a SIMPLE TIME.

A time in which each beat divides into three is called a COMPOUND TIME.

A tune with the time-signature $\frac{2}{4}$ is in SIMPLE DUPLE TIME.

A tune with the time-signature $\frac{6}{8}$ is in COMPOUND DUPLE TIME.

The number of beats in the bar in each case is two (duple time), and each beat lasts for the same duration.

Triplets, then, are used in a piece of music where a group of three notes occurs only occasionally.

Compound time is used when each beat in a piece is regularly divided into three.

In a compound time, with an 8 as the lower figure of the time-signature, one beat is a ♩. In a simple time, with 4 as the lower figure, one beat is a ♩

In both cases the beat lasts for the same length of time.

28

1   2   1   2   1   2   1   2

Summary

A NOTE is a symbol representing the length of a sound.

TABLE OF NOTE VALUES	
1 SEMIBREVE	𝅝
2 MINIMS	𝅗𝅥 𝅗𝅥
4 CROTCHETS	𝅘𝅥 𝅘𝅥 𝅘𝅥 𝅘𝅥
8 QUAVERS	𝅘𝅥𝅮𝅘𝅥𝅮 𝅘𝅥𝅮𝅘𝅥𝅮 𝅘𝅥𝅮𝅘𝅥𝅮 𝅘𝅥𝅮𝅘𝅥𝅮
16 SEMIQUAVERS	𝅘𝅥𝅯𝅘𝅥𝅯𝅘𝅥𝅯𝅘𝅥𝅯 𝅘𝅥𝅯𝅘𝅥𝅯𝅘𝅥𝅯𝅘𝅥𝅯 𝅘𝅥𝅯𝅘𝅥𝅯𝅘𝅥𝅯𝅘𝅥𝅯 𝅘𝅥𝅯𝅘𝅥𝅯𝅘𝅥𝅯𝅘𝅥𝅯

A DOT placed after a note or rest makes it half as long again.

A DOUBLE DOT increases by half again the length of extra time added by one dot (i.e. it increases its length by three quarters).

RESTS are symbols representing the length of periods of silence. There is an equivalent to each note; rests may also be dotted or double-dotted.

The BEAT or PULSE is the regular 'throb' of a piece of music.

RHYTHM is the pattern created by the lengths of the notes (and rests) in a piece of music.

An ACCENT is the natural emphasis which often dictates the number of beats in each bar.

A BAR is a grouping of several beats created by the regular occurrence of accents.

TIME describes the number of beats in each bar.

A TIME-SIGNATURE consists of two numbers, the upper showing the number of beats, or units, in a bar, the lower the unit of each beat as a fraction of a semibreve.

A BAR-LINE marks the beginning and end of each bar.

A DOUBLE BAR-LINE marks the end of a piece of music.

A TIE or BIND ties together two notes of the same pitch to give a note equal in length to their combined values.

An UPBEAT is the last beat in a bar which leads into the first beat of the following bar. There is often an upbeat before the first complete bar of a melody.

ALLA BREVE times use the minim as the unit of the beat, not the crotchet. The BREVE is four minims long, twice as long as a semibreve.

A TRIPLET is a group of three notes played in the time normally taken by two of the same kind.

In SIMPLE TIME the beat divides into two.

In COMPOUND TIME the beat divides into three.

Chapter two

More about ties

The need to treat each half of a quadruple-time bar as a separate unit can present a composer with problems if he wants the melody to move on the *unaccented* beats of the bar.

In his Piano Sonata no. 11, Beethoven wanted to write the following succession of notes in **¢** time on unaccented beats:

29

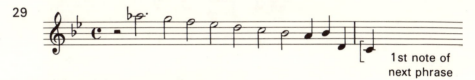

1st note of
next phrase

If you divide the notes and rests into bars of four crotchets, or their equivalent, this is the result:

30

This does not work in **¢** time, as each bar would have an empty beat at the beginning and a minim trying to squeeze itself into one crotchet beat at the end!

31

Try tapping the rhythm.

Beethoven solved his problem by dividing the minims into the equivalent number of crotchets where necessary. Then the whole thing becomes quite simple to follow. First, the dotted minim at the beginning is divided into a minim tied to a crotchet, and then the process is simply continued from there.

32

Now try tapping the rhythm.

Phrases and sentences

You may have wondered about the reference to a 'phrase' in ex. 29.

If you think of the notes in music as being like the syllables of a word and the bars like the words themselves, the next largest unit is the phrase, and the larger one still is the sentence. In music, as in any other language, we have PHRASES and SENTENCES. Often a phrase is four bars long and a sentence is eight.

Sometimes the phrases and sentences are linked by way of the words sung to them. In this particular case, in $\frac{2}{4}$ time, they form two-bar phrases:

33

Often, of course, there are no words, but the music itself still forms phrases and sentences.

34

Sousa: *The Liberty Bell*

In both instances, the first phrase seems to need another to complete it. A phrase is often shown by a PHRASE MARK like this:

35

Mendelssohn: *Pilgrims' March*

More notes and rests

We met the **breve** ‖O‖ in Chapter one as the note equalling four minim beats.

At the other end of the time-scale, the DEMISEMIQUAVER ♫ is half the length of a semiquaver (a quarter of a quaver, an eighth of a crotchet . . . and so on). A demisemiquaver rest ══𝄿══ has the same number of tails as a ♫ .

You may come across even shorter notes, but they are rare. You can tell their duration from the number of tails fastened to their stems: with each extra tail you halve the length of the note.

Hints on: *Add the missing bar-lines to the following extract.*

Beethoven

STEP 1 The time-signature will be provided. Read through the notes from the beginning of the extract. The note-grouping will decide whether the time is simple or compound. A rest, or rests, before the first note shows that the first bar is a complete bar. Suspect an incomplete first bar if there are unexpected note-groupings at the beginning and end of the extract. The accent may be quite clear, and you might realise immediately where the bar-lines should be.

STEP 2 If the accent is not clear, look for longer notes than normal. These will probably be at the ends of phrases. Certainly some of them will be. Starting at one of these long notes, accent the note as though it were at the beginning of a bar and continue accenting notes on the first beats of the following bars in accordance with the time-signature.

STEP 3 If it doesn't feel natural and right as you hear it in your head, first check that you really are conforming to the time-signature and are making the bars the correct length. If you are, start STEP 2 again, but from the note a beat before the one you used in your earlier attempt.

STEP 4 Once either STEP 2 or STEP 3 seems to make musical sense, lightly pencil in the bar-lines.

STEP 5 Having pencilled them in to the end, work backwards from your last pencilled bar-line, grouping the notes and rests into bars of the correct length. (Occasionally you may be able to work backwards from a printed bar-line at the end, cutting out all the previous steps.)

STEP 6 Check the printed note-groupings. You can be sure these are correct and will conform to all the rules about grouping notes and rests by the bar. If a dotted note lasts into the following bar, or a rest seems to make a bar last for an extra beat, you need to attack the problem again.

STEP 7 Now read through the whole extract, and if it seems correct ink in the bar-lines. If you feel there is something wrong, leave it, and come back to this question after you have attempted the rest of the paper. Start again at STEP 1.

Summary

A PHRASE is composed of a small number of bars (often four), and is the equivalent of a phrase in spoken language.

A PHRASE MARK is often used to show the length of a phrase.

A SENTENCE normally consists of two phrases.

A DEMISEMIQUAVER is half the length of a semiquaver, or an eighth of a crotchet.

Chapter three

More about times

We have already looked at several types of duple time. The one thing they all have in common is their constant two beats in a bar:

in **simple duple**　$\frac{2}{4}$　each beat is written as a

in **simple duple**　¢ ($\frac{2}{2}$)　each beat is written as a

in **compound duple**　$\frac{6}{8}$　each beat is written as a

The note showing the basic pulse gives no indication of the TEMPO or speed of the pulse. It is simply the composer's choice.

Compound duple is therefore sometimes written with a basic beat, shown as $\frac{6}{4}$;

36

or with a basic beat, shown as $\frac{6}{16}$.

37

The two examples sound exactly the same, played at the same tempo, but ex. 36 looks much slower than ex. 37.

Grouping of notes

In any time, simple or compound, regardless of the unit of the beat, notes and rests should always be grouped so as to make each beat as clear as possible. This sometimes leads to quite unusual groupings. In quadruple times the halfway point of the bar should also be made clear.

Here are some dos and don'ts:

38

(A whole bar's rest in *every* time except $\frac{4}{2}$)

Hints on: *Rewrite the following extract, grouping the notes correctly.*

Beethoven

STEP 1 The time-signature and bar-lines will be given. You can therefore treat each bar separately. Read through the extract. Most incorrect groupings will be obvious as you will find it difficult to follow the rhythms at these points.

2 beats in a bar – each beat has 3 ♪ s

count 3 ♪ s back from bar-line to find second beat

STEP 2 Recognise where each beat comes, and if necessary mark them lightly in pencil. In bars of compound times with many notes you may also wish to mark each quaver in the same way.

STEP 3 Remember the golden rules:
group by beat;
in quadruple times show the half-bar;
in compound times show that each beat divides into three.

STEP 4 Don't be amazed by some of the printed groupings. The examiner is testing you, after all. Keep cool – and remember, after inking in your reworking of the passage, to erase your pencil marks!

 Now look up this Rondo from the Piano Sonata no. 19 in a volume of Beethoven's sonatas. Why do you think he grouped the notes in such an unconventional way?

Accent and syncopation

In any **duple** time   the accent falls on the **first** beat of each bar.

In any **triple** time   the accent falls on the **first** beat of the bar.

In any **quadruple** time   the main accent falls on the **first** beat of the bar with a less pronounced accent on the **third** beat.

If an accent is on any other part of the bar, the result is SYNCOPATION.

We came across one method of creating syncopation in ex. 32, from Beethoven's Piano Sonata no. 14. Here, since none of the notes in the first four bars is played on an accented beat, the accent is nudged on to beats which are normally unaccented. Tied notes and rests, the methods Beethoven used, are common ways of causing syncopation. But rests may be used on their own, without ties:

39

Tchaikovsky: Waltz

Often a combination of these methods is used.

40

Franck: Symphony

Notice how the composer has written the rhythm of the first four bars ♩ ♩ ♩ , making the syncopation as clear to the eyes as to the ear.

A composer can ask the performer to accent *any* note, just by writing a > above or below it. The sign is itself called an ACCENT.
It can also be used when the performer is required to give a normally accented note even stronger stress.

Summary

TEMPO is the speed of the pulse or beat of a piece of music.
ACCENT is the natural emphasis which often dictates the number of beats in each bar; in duple time it falls on the first beat in each bar; in triple time it falls on the first beat in each bar; in quadruple time it falls on the first beat in each bar with a lesser accent on the third beat.
SYNCOPATION is the displacement of an accented note to an unaccented part of the bar. It can be achieved by: the use of tied notes; rests; an accent sign > ; or a combination of any of these methods.

Chapter four

Times continued

Remember, each beat of a simple time is divided into two; each beat of a compound time is divided into three. So far, the only compound time we have used is compound duple. But each simple time has its matching compound time. Here is a table showing this:

TIME-SIGNATURE		BEATS IN EACH BAR
$\frac{2}{4}$	is simple duple time	
$\frac{6}{8}$	is compound duple time	
$\frac{3}{4}$	is simple triple time	
$\frac{9}{8}$	is compound triple time	
$\frac{4}{4}$	is simple quadruple time	
$\frac{12}{8}$	is compound quadruple time	

41   Here are bars in each time-signature:

Each beat in each bar, simple or compound, lasts the same length of time. The accents, too, fall in the same places in a bar of compound time as in a bar of simple time with the same number of beats.

Below are some Victorian songs in simple and compound times with their natural accents marked:

42

Tat-ters, with his *lit* - tle broom, *Stan*ds a- mid the *crowd*,

Lane: *Tatters*

The *moon* has rais'd her *lamp* a-bove, To *light* the way to *thee*, my love

Benedict: *The Moon has Rais'd her Lamp Above*

Do not *trust* him, gen-tle *la*-dy, Though his *voice* be low and *sweet*.

Goard: *The Gipsy's Warning*

Beau – ti – ful dream – er, *wake* un – to me. ____

Foster: *Beautiful Dreamer*

Yes, let me like a *sol*-dier fall, Up-*on* some o – pen *plain*.

Wallace: *Yes, let me like a soldier fall*

O ___ for the wings, for the *wings* _ of a dove!

Mendelssohn: *O for the Wings of a Dove!*

italics strong accent   . . . . weak accent

Time-signatures with the lower number 4 (indicating a ♩ beat) are most often used in simple times. For those using a ♩ for each beat the lower number is 2, as in $\frac{2}{2}$, simple duple. There is one simple time-signature with the lower number 8. This is $\frac{3}{8}$ and is used when each bar contains three ♪ ♪ ♪ or their equivalent. It is sometimes used as an alternative to $\frac{3}{4}$, and like all simple times each beat can be divided into two, here with two ♫

In compound times, the lower number 8 (showing that each beat divides into ♪♪♪) is the most common. Where the beat divides into ♩ ♩ ♩ the lower number is not 8 but 4 (for example $\frac{6}{4}$, compound duple, in which each bar equals ♩. ♩.). There are also compound times where each beat divides into ♬ . These are indicated by the lower number 16, as there are sixteen ♪s in a semi-breve. $\frac{6}{16}$ ♪. ♪. is a compound duple time.

Here is a table of time-signatures you are likely to meet:

		SIMPLE				COMPOUND			
DUPLE (2 beats)	$\frac{2}{2}$ or ¢	♩	♩			$\frac{6}{4}$	♩.	♩.	
	$\frac{2}{4}$	♩	♩			$\frac{6}{8}$	♩.	♩.	
	$\frac{2}{8}$	♪	♪ [rare]			$\frac{6}{16}$	♪.	♪.	
TRIPLE (3 beats)	$\frac{3}{2}$	♩	♩	♩		$\frac{9}{4}$	♩.	♩.	♩. [rare]
	$\frac{3}{4}$	♩	♩	♩		$\frac{9}{8}$	♩.	♩.	♩.
	$\frac{3}{8}$	♪	♪	♪		$\frac{9}{16}$	♪.	♪.	♪.
QUADRUPLE (4 beats)	$\frac{4}{2}$	♩	♩	♩	♩	$\frac{12}{4}$ ♩. ♩. ♩. ♩. [rare]			
	$\frac{4}{4}$ or C	♩	♩	♩	♩	$\frac{12}{8}$ ♩. ♩. ♩. ♩.			
	$\frac{4}{8}$	♪	♪	♪	♪ [rare]	$\frac{12}{16}$ ♪. ♪. ♪. ♪.			

More complicated music uses many more time-signatures. As long ago as 1913 Stravinsky composed *The Rite of Spring* which makes use of many of the more unusual ones. Here is a typical succession of its time-signatures:

$\frac{5}{8}$ | $\frac{9}{8}$ | $\frac{5}{8}$ | $\frac{7}{8}$ | $\frac{3}{8}$ | $\frac{2}{4}$ | $\frac{7}{4}$ | $\frac{3}{4}$ | $\frac{7}{8}$

A bar of $\frac{7}{8}$ or $\frac{5}{4}$ normally consists of two bars of other times. In Tchaikovsky's Sixth Symphony, for example, there is a tune in $\frac{5}{4}$; it is really a combination of $\frac{2}{4}$ + $\frac{3}{4}$ in each bar. Notice how the composer has made this clear in the notation.

43

Tchaikovsky: Symphony no. 6

The duplet

Just as in a simple time we can use a triplet for the occasional beat we need to divide into three, so in a compound time we may use a DUPLET when we wish to divide a beat into two.

We simply take two notes, each the length of the three normally making up a beat (or their equivalent), and group them under a ⌐2¬.

quaver duplets in $\frac{6}{8}$:

44

crotchet duplets in $\frac{6}{4}$:

Summary

$\frac{2}{2}$ (¢) and $\frac{2}{4}$ are SIMPLE DUPLE TIMES.

$\frac{6}{4}$, $\frac{6}{8}$ and $\frac{6}{16}$ are COMPOUND DUPLE TIMES.

In duple time each bar contains two beats, with an accent on the first.

$\frac{3}{2}$, $\frac{3}{4}$ and $\frac{3}{8}$ are SIMPLE TRIPLE TIMES.

$\frac{9}{8}$ and $\frac{9}{16}$ are COMPOUND TRIPLE TIMES.

In triple time each bar contains three beats, with an accent on the first.

$\frac{4}{2}$ and $\frac{4}{4}$ (C) are SIMPLE QUADRUPLE TIMES.

$\frac{12}{8}$ and $\frac{12}{16}$ are COMPOUND QUADRUPLE TIMES.

In quadruple time each bar contains four beats, with the main accent on the first and a lesser accent on the third.

A DUPLET is two notes played in the time of three of the same kind.

Chapter five

More about the rhythms of words

You may be asked to write a rhythm on one note to fit given words. You should give the correct time-signature and bar-lines.

Bear in mind that very few songs begin on the first beat of the bar. A glance through any book of songs, whether folk-songs or the works of a composer, will show this.

By now you should be fairly good at spotting the accented syllables in verse. Always read the given verse several times and underline the accented syllables before even starting to decide on the time-signature. You should also realise that there may be more than one correct way of setting words to music.

Look at these typical extracts:

> I *have* a *wid*owed *mother who*
> Would *be* the *very thing* for *you.*   W. S. Gilbert

> In *Xanadu* did *Kubla Khan*
> A *stately plea*sure *dome* de*cree.*   S. T. Coleridge

In both, the accents fall on alternating syllables. They could therefore both be written in $\frac{2}{4}$.

But look at the character of the extracts.

The couplet by Gilbert (from *Captain Reece*) is obviously light-hearted. As Sullivan knew well, a great deal of Gilbert's verse feels very much like $\frac{6}{8}$:

45

I *have* a *wi*-dowed *mo*-ther *who* Would *be* the *ve* -ry   *thing* for *you.*

The extract from Coleridge's *Kubla Khan* is more spacious, serious, thoughtful and imaginative. Frequent accents should be avoided in setting words of this type. They're not the sort of words you would chant to a skipping-game!

$\frac{4}{4}$, with its main and subsidiary accents, is more appropriate than $\frac{2}{4}$ or $\frac{6}{8}$.

46
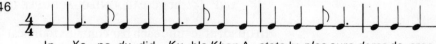

In   *Xa* - na-*du* did   *Ku*- bla *Khan* A   *state*-ly *plea*-sure *dome* de-*cree.*

Be careful when setting-out combinations of music and words.

Write the words first. They usually take more space than the notes. Always divide syllables with a hyphen. If there are double letters between syllables (happen) the hyphen goes between them (hap-pen). If a word is made from two other words (outlook), the hyphen comes between them (out-look). Otherwise the rule is that normally the hyphen comes before a consonant (ci-vi-li-sa-tion). The exceptions are words ending with '-ing, '-ist, '-ism', and so forth.

Be sure the syllable is precisely under the note to which it is to be sung. If the note is long, the syllable is written at the beginning:

e – xa – mi – na – tion

Checklist

By now you should have become confident in the following aspects of rhythm:

note values from ‖◌‖ to ♪ with equivalent rests
dotted notes and rests
double-dotted notes and rests
tied notes
simple duple, triple and quadruple times
compound duple, triple and quadruple times
triplets and duplets
groupings of notes and rests
adding time-signatures to passages of music
barring unbarred passages of music
accent and syncopation
adding a rhythm on one note to fit given words